STUDY GUIDE

PASSOVER TO PENTECOST

50 Days that Changed the World

ROBERT MORRIS

Passover to Pentecost Study Guide
Copyright © 2023 by Robert Morris

Content taken from "Passover to Pentecost" sermons delivered in 2021 by Robert Morris at Gateway Church, Southlake, TX.

Unless otherwise noted, Scripture taken from the New King James Version®. Copyright © 1982 by Thomas Nelson. Used by permission. All rights reserved.

Scripture quotations marked (ESV) are taken from the ESV® Bible (The Holy Bible, English Standard Version®), copyright © 2001 by Crossway, a publishing ministry of Good News Publishers. Used by permission. All rights reserved.

Scripture quotations marks (KJV) are taken from the King James Version of the Bible. Public domain.

Scripture quotations marked (MSG) are taken from THE MESSAGE, copyright © 1993, 2002, 2018 by Eugene H. Peterson. Used by permission of NavPress, represented by Tyndale House Publishers. All rights reserved.

Scripture quotations marked (NIV) are taken from the Holy Bible, New International Version®, NIV®. Copyright © 1973, 1978, 1984, 2011 by Biblica, Inc.™ Used by permission of Zondervan. All rights reserved worldwide. www.zondervan.com. The "NIV" and "New International Version" are trademarks registered in the United States Patent and Trademark Office by Biblica, Inc.™

All rights reserved. No portion of this publication may be reproduced, stored in a retrieval system, or transmitted in any form by any means—electronic, mechanical, photocopying, recording, or any other—without prior permission from the publisher. "Gateway Publishing" and "Gateway Press" are trademarks registered in the United States Patent and Trademark Office by Gateway Church.

ISBN: 978-1-951227-84-5 Paperback
ISBN: 978-1-951227-85-2 eBook
ISBN: 978-1-951227-86-9 Companion DVD

We hope you hear from the Holy Spirit and receive God's richest blessings from this book by Gateway Publishing. Gateway Publishing's purpose is to carry out the mission and vision of Gateway Church through print and digital resources to equip leaders, disciple believers, and advance God's Kingdom.

Gateway Press, an imprint of Gateway Publishing
700 Blessed Way
Southlake, Texas 76092
GatewayPublishing.com

Printed in the United States of America
23 24 25 26 27—5 4 3 2 1

CONTENTS

Welcome   1

Introduction   3

SESSION 1
Passover   7

SESSION 2
According to the Flesh   31

SESSION 3
Benefits of the Resurrection   55

SESSION 4
Believe   79

SESSION 5
Waiting for the Promise   105

SESSION 6
Pentecost   131

Leader's Guide   153

About the Author   159

WELCOME

Welcome to the *Passover to Pentecost Study Guide*! I am so glad you've chosen to explore and learn more about the 50 days between Jesus' death on the cross and the outpouring of the Holy Spirit at Pentecost. There is much Jesus said and did in this short period of time that is encouraging and helpful for us today.

Whether you use this study guide as part of a small group experience or individual study, I know your faith and relationship with the Lord will grow. My prayer is that you will be blessed and "grow in the grace and knowledge of our Lord and Savior Jesus Christ" (2 Peter 3:18) as you discover more about the 50 days that changed the world!

Robert Morris
Senior Pastor, Gateway Church

INTRODUCTION

This study guide has a simple design with easy-to-follow section headings.

ENGAGE

This section provides an icebreaker question for small groups to help people begin engaging with one another and feeling comfortable sharing in a group setting.

RECAP

Beginning with the second message, this section briefly summarizes the previous message.

WATCH/READ

There is something powerful about hearing the message and gathering with other believers, even through digital devices, so watch the message if possible. If you're unable to watch, the Read section provides a comprehensive review of the message.

REFLECT

These open-ended questions help you reflect on Scripture and the truths you learned in the message. Write your answers in the space provided. If you are in a group and feel comfortable doing so, consider sharing your answers with others.

PRAY

This is a time to ask, "Holy Spirit, what are You saying to me through this message?" Then listen for His answer and allow Him to direct the message to you personally. Write down what you hear Him saying to you. If you are in a group, take some time to pray for each other.

EXPLORE

This section offers key quotes, additional questions, and Scriptures to memorize, meditate on, and write about throughout the week. There is also a guided prayer to seal in your heart all the Lord has done and spoken to you through the message.

SESSION 1

PASSOVER

SESSION 1

PASSOVER

Passover reminds us of when the angel of death passed over the homes marked with the blood of the lamb. The Feast of Passover included unleavened bread and firstfruits, and Jesus fulfilled both at Passover. Jesus is the unleavened bread and firstfruits offering.

ENGAGE

What holidays have special or spiritual significance for you?

_____

_____

_____

_____

_____

_____

_____

_____

WATCH

Watch "Passover." Think about how the early church celebrated Passover. Consider what Passover means for believers today.

> If you're unable to watch this message, skip to the Read section.

NOTES

_____
_____
_____
_____
_____
_____
_____
_____
_____
_____
_____

READ

In *Passover to Pentecost: 50 Days that Changed the World,* I share about the 50 days between Passover (when Jesus died on the cross) and Pentecost (when the Holy Spirit was given to the early believers). After Jesus rose from death, He spent 40 days on the earth. Then He ascended into heaven, and the disciples spent 10 days fasting and seeking God until Pentecost. The first four messages in this series address the 40 days, and the final two messages address the 10 days leading up to Pentecost.

When we think of "Passover," we often think of a single day on the Jewish calendar—the 14th or 15th day of Nisan, which is pronounced 'Nye-San.' Similar to a birthday or Christmas, though, Passover is more than the celebration of a certain calendar day. It's a celebration of what the day represents. Passover was implemented almost 3,500 years ago and was fulfilled by Jesus almost 2,000 years ago. (I will explain more about this in my first point.)

There were three major feasts in Israel: Passover, Pentecost, and Tabernacles. You may have heard that there are seven feasts, which is true. Three feasts are included in Passover (Passover, Unleavened Bread, and Firstfruits). Then there is the Feast of Pentecost. Finally, three feasts are in included in Tabernacles (Trumpets, the Day of Atonement, and Tabernacles).

The three feasts of Passover happened the weekend of Passover 2,000 years ago, and Jesus fulfilled all three. Fifty days later on Pentecost, the Holy Spirit came and fulfilled Pentecost. Tabernacles *will* be fulfilled someday. Trumpets represents the Second Coming, the Day of Atonement represents the Judgment Seat, and Tabernacles represents when God "tabernacles" (lives) with us for all eternity in heaven.

Even though you were not alive when Jesus was on this earth and fulfilled Passover, you can partake in the fulfillment of Passover, Unleavened Bread, and Firstfruits by receiving Jesus as your Savior. Even though you weren't alive at the time of Acts 2 when the Holy Spirit came, you can partake in the fulfillment of Pentecost by allowing the Holy Spirit to take control of your life. Even though you may not be alive when Jesus returns, if you believe in Him, you will partake in the Feasts of Trumpets, Atonement, and Tabernacles.

By the way, I don't often preach about the end times, because there are many different views. I do know two things for sure, though. First, Jesus will return. Second, no one knows when (see Matthew 24:36). I once heard Pastor Jack Hayford jokingly say, "I've thought many times, *I wonder if some people have figured it out, and the Lord had to move it.*" We know Jesus *will* return, but we are not meant to live focused only on that. Many people get so caught up on this topic, like the disciples did, but Jesus said, "It's not for you to know" (see Acts 1:7). Instead, we should be concerned about winning people to Jesus.

Three times each year, God brought Israel together for planting, firstfruits, and harvest. So what does the word Passover mean? Passover comes from two words put together: "pass" and "over." We see this combination in Exodus 12:23:

> For the Lord will pass through to strike the Egyptians; and when He sees the blood on the lintel and on the two doorposts, the Lord will **pass over** the door and

> not allow the destroyer to come into your houses to strike *you* (bold added).

Do you realize what good news this is? The Lord will not allow the destroyer to come into your house! That's what we're celebrating when we celebrate Passover—the resurrection of Jesus Christ. Exodus 12:23 refers to the 10th and final plague God brought against Egypt. Every plague was a judgment on the 10 major gods and goddesses of Egypt. This is explained in Numbers 33:4: "On their gods the Lord had executed judgments." In every plague, it was as if God was saying, "No, you aren't the god of water. I'm the God of water, and I can turn water into blood. No, you aren't the god of animals or light and darkness. I control those things! And no, you aren't the god of life. I control life."

> Now the blood shall be a sign for you on the houses where you *are*. And when I see the blood, I will **pass over** you; and the plague shall not be on you to destroy *you* when I strike the land of Egypt (Exodus 12:13, bold added).

Notice that God said the blood would be a sign to "you"—the people. I would have thought that the blood was a sign for God to pass over their houses. However, God doesn't need an outward sign, because He knows the heart. It took faith to kill the lamb and put its blood on the doorposts. It took faith to do a lot of things God told Israel to do. Again, God knows what's in your heart. *The blood of Jesus is a sign to us that the destroyer cannot come into our houses!* The plague cannot come into our homes!

When the word Passover is used in Scripture, it is referring to one of three subjects: the Festival, the Meal, or the Lamb.

THE FESTIVAL

> So this day shall be to you a memorial; and you shall keep it as a feast to the Lord throughout your generations. You shall keep it as a feast by an everlasting ordinance (Exodus 12:14).

Feast is the root word of festival. Passover is the Jewish festival that begins at sundown on the fifteenth day of Nisan. It lasts for seven days in Israel (or eight days outside Israel). The Passover celebration begins on the first evening (or first two evenings outside Israel) with the meal known as the seder. The Exodus story is read during the meal, and special foods represent elements of the story. No work is permitted on the first and last days of the Passover Festival.

In Matthew 26:2, Jesus says, "You know that after two days is the Passover, and the Son of Man will be delivered up to be crucified." Here, Jesus is referring to the festival. God wanted His people to come together to celebrate and feast. There is a lot of preaching on fasting, and while this is good and important, feasting is also good and important.

> And the Lord spoke to Moses, saying, "Speak to the children of Israel, and say to them: 'When you come into the land which I give to you, and reap its harvest, then you shall bring a sheaf of the firstfruits of your harvest to the priest. He shall wave the sheaf before the Lord, to be accepted on your behalf; on the day after the Sabbath the priest shall wave it'" (Leviticus 23:9–11).

The Israelites were to bring their firstfruits (Festival of Firstfruits), *which the priest would wave on the day after the Sabbath.* Jesus was crucified on Passover, laid in the tomb on the Sabbath, and resurrected on the day after the Sabbath.

The New Testament fulfillment of these first three feasts is shown in 1 Corinthians:

> Therefore purge out the old leaven, that you may be a new lump, since you truly are unleavened. For indeed Christ, our Passover, was sacrificed for us (5:7).

> But now Christ is risen from the dead, *and* has become the firstfruits of those who have fallen asleep (15:20).

On Passover, the father of the house takes three pieces of unleavened bread (think of Father, Son, and Holy Spirit). Then he takes the middle piece, breaks it, wraps it in a cloth (like Jesus' body after He was crucified), and hides it. Early in the morning on the day after the Sabbath, the children go looking for the middle piece of bread. When they find it, they unwrap it and wave it before the Lord as a firstfruits offering. Jesus was sacrificed on Passover, wrapped in a cloth, and brought out at sunrise the day after the Sabbath. He fulfilled every Scripture about Passover! Jesus is our Passover, our Unleavened Bread, and our Firstfruits.

THE MEAL

> And thus you shall eat it: *with* a belt on your waist, your sandals on your feet, and your staff in your hand. So you shall eat it in haste. It *is* the Lord's Passover (Exodus 12:11).

> Then He said to them, "With *fervent* desire I have desired to eat this Passover with you before I suffer" (Luke 22:15).

These Scriptures refer to eating the meal, not the day. As I mentioned before, the Passover meal (seder) involves unique foods that represent elements of the Exodus story. Bitter herbs (usually horseradish) represent the bitterness of slavery. Unleavened bread (*matzo*) is also eaten because the people didn't have time to prepare regular bread as they fled. During the Last Supper, Jesus speaks about His body and blood:

> And as they were eating, Jesus took bread, blessed and broke *it,* and gave *it* to the disciples and said, "Take, eat; this is My body."
>
> Then He took the cup, and **gave thanks**, and gave *it* to them, saying, "Drink from it, all of you. For this is My blood of the new covenant, which is shed for many for the remission of sins" (Matthew 26:26–28, bold added).

"Gave thanks" is the Greek word *eucharisteo*, which is where we get our English word Eucharist.

Three years earlier, during the beginning of His ministry, Jesus made a very strong statement that many people do not understand to this day: "Most assuredly, I say to you, unless you eat the flesh of the Son of Man and drink His blood, you have no life in you" (John 6:53). This verse isn't referring to the Lord's Supper—the Lord's Supper does not save you. You cannot live a horrible, sinful life and simply eat a wafer and drink some juice and be saved. Now, is this a type of communion? Yes, it certainly is, but this verse is actually referring to salvation.

Reading the Bible is like going on a treasure hunt; it is so fun to search for things and find treasure in Scripture. The Bible is a spiritual book written by a Spirit to spirits. If you try to understand it with your natural mind, you will never succeed. But if you'll search the Scriptures, then you will see all sorts of treasure.

Not too long ago, my wife, Debbie, and I went on a scavenger hunt with some friends. I am happy to report that our team won! Debbie and the wife of one of our elders figured out every clue! The first clue was this:

After you've done Proverbs 24:3, you might want to go here to fill it. You can also get fudge and popcorn here. And you can mail a letter here, but it's not the Post Office.

I knew that Proverbs 24:3 talks about wisdom building a house, but Debbie knew where you could get furniture, fudge, and popcorn *and* mail a letter. She immediately said, "Weir's Furniture!" She was right, and we eventually won the game.

Whenever you're trying to find out the meaning of something in Scripture, you need to read the context. What does Jesus mean about eating His flesh and drinking His blood? John 6:56 provides the context: "He who eats My flesh and drinks My blood abides in Me, and I in him." The key to understanding this verse is abiding. *Whoever does this abides in Me, and I in him.* There are two abidings. How do I abide in God? The answer is found in 1 John 4:15: "Whoever confesses that Jesus is the Son of God, God abides in him, and he in God."

You eat His body and drink His blood by confessing that Jesus is the Son of God. As we see in Matthew 10:32, that confession must be a public confession:

"Therefore whoever confesses Me before men, him I will also confess before My Father who is in heaven." Don't try to be a secret disciple. Jesus died for you publicly, so you need to live for Him publicly.

I used to preach crusades, and I will never forget one night when I preached to a large group of young people (many of whom were athletes). The head cheerleader begged her boyfriend, the captain of the football team, to come forward and give his life to Christ. He said, "No, I'm going to have fun first." He died later that night in a car accident. You aren't guaranteed tomorrow. I am begging you to confess Jesus as the Son of God publicly *today*. That's the only way you're going to have life!

THE LAMB

> Then Moses called for all the elders of Israel and said to them, "Pick out and take lambs for yourselves according to your families, and kill the Passover *lamb*" (Exodus 12:21).
>
> Then came the Day of Unleavened Bread, when the Passover must be killed (Luke 22:7).

These verses are obviously not referring to a day or meal. John 1:29 says this is clearly about Jesus:

> The next day John saw Jesus coming toward him, and said, "Behold! The Lamb of God who takes away the sin of the world!"

The Passover lamb was to be set apart from the other lambs on the 10th day of Nisan, four days before Passover. On the 10th day of Nisan, Jesus entered Jerusalem. What we call the triumphal entry was when Jesus was being separated so that He would be the sacrifice.

Look at Exodus 12:7:

> And they shall take *some* of the blood and put *it* on the two doorposts and on the lintel of the houses where they eat it.

They placed blood on the two sides of the door and on the lintel (mantle) above it. The blood dripped down in four places, creating the outline of a cross. Now think about Jesus—the nails in His hands, the crown of thorns on His head, and the nail in His feet. Jesus Christ is the Passover Lamb.

As a believer, you need to know that the blood of Jesus stands guard at your door, and the destroyer cannot come into your house to get your family. Jesus is at your door!

NOTES

REFLECT

1. Why do you think God likes it when His people come together to celebrate?

_____

_____

_____

_____

_____

_____

2. What does the word Passover mean, and why is it important to us today?

_____

_____

_____

_____

_____

_____

3. Why do you think the priest would inspect the lamb and not the man who brought the lamb? What does that mean for us as we think about Jesus, the Lamb of God?

_____

_____

_____

_____

_____

_____

_____

4. Read Matthew 10:32–33. Why is it important for believers to make a public confession of faith?

_____

_____

_____

_____

_____

_____

_____

5. Read Exodus 12:7. What does it mean to you that the blood on the doorposts formed a cross?

PRAY

Spend some time in prayer and ask the Holy Spirit, "What are You saying to me through this message?"

EXPLORE

KEY QUOTE

> *The blood of Jesus is a sign to us that the destroyer cannot come into our houses.*

How does it make you feel to know that you are protected by the blood of Jesus?

_____

_____

_____

_____

_____

_____

KEY VERSES

Exodus 12:7, 11, 13–14

Matthew 10:32–33; 26:2

Luke 22:15

John 6:56

1 Corinthians 5:7

What truths stand out to you as you read these verses?

_____

_____

_____

What is the Holy Spirit saying to you through these Scriptures?

_____

_____

_____

KEY QUESTION

Have you made a public confession of your faith in Christ? If not, would you like to do so now? If you have, how can your life represent Christ on a daily basis?

_____

_____

_____

_____

_____

KEY PRAYER

Heavenly Father, thank You for Jesus. Thank You for giving us the firstfruit of Christ, who takes away our sins. We confess that Jesus Christ is the Son of God and our Savior. We thank You that through the blood of Jesus, death has passed over us, and we receive Your gift of everlasting life. In Jesus' name, Amen.

NOTES

SESSION 2

ACCORDING TO THE FLESH

SESSION 2

ACCORDING TO THE FLESH

The Bible tells us not to regard any person according to the flesh. We should never judge anyone by their ethnicity, gender, age, or appearance. Instead, we should get to know people as God made them and by their spirit.

ENGAGE

Why does society tend to judge someone on the outside before getting to know them on the inside?

_____
_____
_____
_____
_____
_____
_____
_____

RECAP

In the previous message, we learned that the three feasts of Passover point us to Jesus' death, burial, and resurrection. Jesus is our Passover Lamb. We can partake in the fulfillment of Passover today by receiving Him as our Lord and Savior. How did you see Jesus' death, burial, and resurrection in a new way this past week?

WATCH

Watch "According to the Flesh." Think about the ways we tend to prejudge people. Consider how the Bible says we should get to know people.

> If you're unable to watch this message, skip to the Read section.

NOTES

READ

Do you know what happened after the resurrection? This may surprise you, but after Jesus rose again, His followers did not recognize Him.

> But Mary stood outside by the tomb weeping, and as she wept she stooped down *and looked* into the tomb. And she saw two angels in white sitting, one at the head and the other at the feet, where the body of Jesus had lain. Then they said to her, "Woman, why are you weeping?"
>
> She said to them, "Because they have taken away my Lord, and I do not know where they have laid Him."
>
> Now when she had said this, she turned around and saw Jesus standing *there,* and did not know that it was Jesus (John 20:11–14).

Doesn't it seem strange that Mary didn't know Jesus? She had been with Him for what many believe to be most (if not all) of His ministry years.

> Then, the same day at evening, being the first *day* of the week, when the doors were shut where the disciples were assembled, for fear of the Jews, Jesus came and stood in the midst, and said to them, "Peace

be with you." When He had said this, He showed them *His* hands and His side. Then the disciples were glad when they saw the Lord....

Then He said to Thomas, "Reach your finger here, and look at My hands; and reach your hand *here,* and put *it* into My side. Do not be unbelieving, but believing."

And Thomas answered and said to Him, "My Lord and my God!" (John 20:19–20, 27–28).

You would think that walking through the wall would have been enough for the disciples to recognize Jesus, but even after He spoke to them, they didn't recognize Him. In verse 28, Thomas only recognized Jesus after Thomas put his hand in Jesus' side.

Luke 24 tells us about two of Jesus' followers who were traveling to the village of Emmaus and how Jesus joined them on their journey. He walked and talked with them for hours, yet the two men did not recognize Jesus until later.

Now it came to pass, as He sat at the table with them, that He took bread, blessed and broke *it,* and gave it to them. Then their eyes were opened and they knew Him; and He vanished from their sight (Luke 24:30–31).

Isn't that amazing? These men had been with Jesus for three and a half years, but it wasn't until "their eyes were opened" that they realized it was Him.

Now, let's look at 2 Corinthians 5:16–17:

> Therefore, from now on, we regard no one according to the flesh. Even though we have known Christ according to the flesh, yet now we know *Him thus* no longer. Therefore, if anyone *is* in Christ, *he is* a new creation; old things have passed away; behold, all things have become new.

Many believers are familiar with verse 17. In verse 16 Paul says that we once knew Christ "according to the flesh," because He became human and walked on the earth for 33 years. We don't know Him that way any longer, and as believers, we also must decide not to regard others according to the flesh.

What does Jesus look like? Now, I didn't ask, "What *did* Jesus look like?" When you imagine Jesus, do you imagine a human form? Of course you do, and there's nothing wrong with that. But if we imagine Jesus in a human form, aren't we knowing Him according to the flesh?

I started my television program in 2007, so now people recognize me when they see me because they have seen my face. But prior to that, my book *The Blessed Life* came out in 2001, followed by *Dream to Destiny* and *Power of Your Words*. Since the Internet wasn't as popular back then, when people read my books or listened to my CDs, they had to imagine what I looked like. Whenever I traveled and preached at different churches, I would begin by saying, "You don't look like I thought you would either!" Many people had imagined me as an older man, and back then, I was still young!

When I was growing up, my grandmother had a picture of Jesus on her wall. He had light skin, long and wavy hair down to His shoulders, and a short beard and mustache. I thought she took it herself! He almost looked Swedish. Other depictions of Jesus give him a much darker complexion. The *Jesus* film used various representations of Jesus with different ethnicities so different cultures could relate to Him. My point is this: we don't know what Jesus looked like, and when we imagine Him, we imagine Him "according to the flesh."

What if we did what Paul said and no longer regarded Jesus according to the flesh? What if I no longer regard you according to what your flesh is? What if I take the time to know you as a person? This is the answer to prejudice in our world.

Let's look at four applications of this truth.

ETHNICITY

Ethnicity comes from the Greek word *ethnos*, which means 'nations, languages, or regions of the world.'

> Then the woman of Samaria said to Him, "How is it that You, being a Jew, ask a drink from me, a Samaritan woman?" For Jews have no dealings with Samaritans.
> Jesus answered and said to her, "If you knew the gift of God, and who it is who says to you, 'Give Me a drink,' you would have asked Him, and He would have given you living water" (John 4:9–10).

Notice the woman at the well brings race into the conversation. What Jesus was saying to her was, "You're judging me after the flesh. You're prejudging me." Prejudice means prejudging, or judging without the facts. All prejudice is prejudgment. Jesus was saying that if this woman could judge Him after the Spirit instead of after the flesh, she would realize that He could give her living water.

All the different ethnicities wouldn't matter. Every human is a person, and every person needs a Savior. We need to get past the issue of race—*ethnos*. If we made that decision, it would completely solve the prejudice problem.

I'm not saying we don't see, notice, or recognize a different ethnicity from ourselves. I'm saying we don't regard others based on that. The word regard means to judge, to get to know, to interview, and to discern. In other words, I'm going to get to know you *not* according to your flesh. I'm going to get to know you as a person.

I have a pastor friend who is African American (I mention this detail only because it is relevant to the story). I got together with him after my daughter, Elaine, married her husband, Ethan. My friend had never met Ethan, so I showed him a picture of the newlyweds. My friend said, "He's black!" I replied, "What?! I met with that guy for six months, and he never told me he is black!" Of course, I was teasing my friend. I knew Ethan's race. I just hadn't mentioned it because it didn't matter to us what his race was. Instead, what mattered was that Elaine loves Ethan, our family loves him, and he is a wonderful man. We don't regard him according to the flesh.

GENDER

Galatians 3:28 addresses race, status, and gender:

> There is neither Jew nor Greek, there is neither slave nor free, there is neither male nor female; for you are all one in Christ Jesus.

In Christ, there is no difference in gender—we are all one. Women are not less competent or intelligent than men because they have different body parts. If you have any negative feelings or thoughts when a woman walks into a business meeting, then you're biased. When you decide not to regard someone according to the flesh, then you're not talking to a female—you're talking to a person.

I realize there are differences between men and women, and we notice those differences. But we can also choose not to judge someone based on those differences. We must get to know that person as a *person*, according to the Spirit and not according to the flesh.

Gender differences are more than just biological or physical factors. For example, studies show that women are more in touch with their emotions than men are. But we should not regard women in a demeaning way just because they're different than men.

AGE

First Timothy 4:12 says, "Let no one despise your youth, but be an example to the believers in word, in conduct, in love, in spirit, in faith, in purity." The word despise comes from the Greek word meaning 'to contemn—to treat or regard someone with contempt, as unworthy of consideration.' This is where we get our English word contempt. Age discrimination is prejudice!

First Timothy 5:1–2 has a phenomenal truth that most people read over and never see:

> Do not rebuke an older man, but exhort *him* as a father, younger men as brothers, older women as mothers, younger women as sisters, with all purity.

Paul first tells Timothy not to rebuke an older man. Even if you need to correct him, exhort him—speak in an honoring way. Treat him as you would a *father*. The next sentence is surprising; he tells older men to treat younger men as *brothers*—not as sons. Likewise, Paul tells the younger women to speak to the older women as *mothers*, and the older women to speak to the younger women as *sisters*.

In other words, it's okay to look up to someone, but it's not okay to look down on anyone. We should respect our elders, but we must not disrespect our youth. Younger men and women are our brothers and sisters in Christ.

I regularly meet with a Christian life coach, and one day my son Josh joined me. The life coach asked, "Josh, who is that sitting on the couch beside you?" Josh answered, "My dad." Then the life coach asked me, "Robert, who is that sitting on the couch beside you?" I said, "My son." Then the life coach replied, "Not according to the Bible. According to the Bible, you two are brothers. Josh, if you see your father as higher than you, and Robert, if you see your son as lower than you, then you two are going to have problems for the rest of your lives." We had to begin to see ourselves as brothers.

APPEARANCE

We don't judge people by ethnicity, gender, age, or appearance. There could be many more applications, but the point is to stop judging people according to the flesh.

God told Samuel to anoint the next king of Israel. He didn't tell the prophet who the man was—only that the king would be one of the sons of Jesse.

> So it was, when they came, that he looked at Eliab and said, "Surely the Lord's anointed *is* before Him!"
> But the Lord said to Samuel, "Do not look at his appearance or at his physical stature, because I have refused him. For *the Lord does* not *see* as man sees; for man looks at the outward appearance, but the Lord looks at the heart" (1 Samuel 16:6–7).

How many times do we judge by someone's outward appearance? Tall, short, thin, heavy-set, long hair, short hair, etc.?

I have a friend who was a professional basketball player. Whenever he meets someone new who says they want to ask him a question, he responds with: "6'9", 13, Yes." The questions he's answering are:

"How tall are you? What size shoe do you wear? Did you play basketball?" I'm not saying it's wrong to notice. You can't help but notice a guy who's 6′9″! But we shouldn't judge someone by their appearance.

As I've stated several times, the point of this message is to teach us to stop regarding others according to the flesh. Let's read a verse about this in the Message version:

> Because of this decision we don't evaluate people by what they have or how they look. We looked at the Messiah that way once and got it all wrong, as you know. We certainly don't look at him that way anymore (2 Corinthians 5:16).

My good friend Nick Vujicic was born with no arms and no legs. When I first met him many years ago, he said four words to me. In fact, every time he meets someone, he says the same four words: "Give me a hug!" You'd make a huge mistake if you judged Nick according to his flesh. He is a wonderful person to get to know and gives great hugs!

It's a huge mistake for us to judge anyone according to the flesh. What if Christians everywhere said,

"From now on, we will not judge people according to the flesh. Instead, we will get to know everyone according to the Spirit"? I believe we would change the world!

NOTES

REFLECT

1. Read John 20:14, 19-20. How is it that Jesus' disciples didn't recognize Him in these verses? What does that show us about making judgments based upon what we see?

2. Read 2 Corinthians 5:16-17. What does it mean not to "regard" anyone according to the flesh?

3. In what ways does our society prejudge others? How does this prejudice bring destruction?

_____
_____
_____
_____
_____
_____
_____

4. Have you ever felt prejudged by someone? How did that make you feel?

_____
_____
_____
_____
_____
_____
_____

5. Read Matthew 7:12. How does the Golden Rule keep us from prejudging others?

PRAY

Spend some time in prayer and ask the Holy Spirit, "What are You saying to me through this message?"

EXPLORE

KEY QUOTE

> *It's okay to look up to someone;*
> *it's not okay to look down on anyone.*

Is there a type of person you look down on? What will you do to change that? How will you begin to regard them by the Spirit?

_____

_____

_____

_____

_____

KEY VERSES

John 20:11–14, 19–20, 26–28
Galatians 3:28
1 Timothy 4:12; 5:1–2
1 Samuel 16:6–7

What truths stand out to you as you read these verses?

_____
_____
_____

What is the Holy Spirit saying to you through these Scriptures?

_____
_____
_____

KEY QUESTION

What would it look like if every Christian took this message to heart and lived every day judging people according to the Spirit?

_____
_____
_____
_____
_____

KEY PRAYER

Heavenly Father, thank You for Your Word. Help us to lay aside prejudice and open our hearts to those who are not like us in the flesh. Please help us to include others and regard one another according to the Spirit. Give us strength and wisdom to stand on Your promises and to love our neighbors as we love ourselves. In Jesus' name, Amen.

NOTES

SESSION 3

BENEFITS OF THE RESURRECTION

SESSION 3

BENEFITS OF THE RESURRECTION

When we believe in Jesus, everything changes. Jesus explains the Bible to us, opens our eyes to the truth, and applies Scriptures to our lives. He blesses us so we can be witnesses for Him and build His Kingdom.

ENGAGE

How did your life change when you first believed in Jesus?

RECAP

In the previous message, we learned that God does not want us to regard others according to the flesh. We should never prejudge people by their ethnicity, gender, age, or appearance. If we lived as the Bible instructs us, there would be no prejudice in the world. Did you find yourself starting to prejudge someone this week based on what you saw or heard? How did you address that tendency to prejudge?

WATCH

Watch "Benefits of the Resurrection." Think about the ways Jesus changes things for His disciples. Consider how you can be a blessing for God's kingdom.

> If you're unable to watch this message, skip to the Read section.

NOTES

READ

Luke 24 and Acts 1 record the ascension of Christ. Jesus was on the earth for 40 days after the resurrection, and then the disciples spent 10 days praying in the Upper Room. Acts 2 records the arrival of the Holy Spirit on the Day of Pentecost.

In this message, I will show you three benefits of the resurrection, all found in Luke 24. This chapter tells the story of the two disciples on the road to Emmaus. Now, these men were not part of the original 12 disciples. We know this because one was named Cleopas (not one of the 12), and the passage says that the two went back and reported to the remaining eleven. Therefore, the second man could not have been one of the original 12 disciples either. They were probably part of the larger group of 70 followers of Christ (see Luke 10:1).

Jesus appears to the two disciples on the road, but they don't recognize Him. He asks what they're talking about, and they wonder why He doesn't know about the current events. Then Jesus does something you need to know is a benefit if you're a disciple.

Then He said to them, "O foolish ones, and slow of heart to believe in all that the prophets have spoken! Ought not the Christ to have suffered these things and to enter into His glory?" And beginning at Moses and all the Prophets, He expounded to them in all the Scriptures the things concerning Himself....

Then He said to them, "These *are* the words which I spoke to you while I was still with you, that all things must be fulfilled which were written in the Law of Moses and *the* Prophets and *the* Psalms concerning Me." And He opened their understanding, that they might comprehend the Scriptures (Luke 24:25–27, 44–45).

HE EXPLAINS

Luke 24:27 is the key verse. "Expounded" simply means explained. Another version of the Bible says, "Beginning with Moses and all the prophets, he explained to them" (NIV). Jesus explained all the Scriptures about Himself. Here's what I want you to understand: *If you're a disciple and believe in Jesus, He will explain the Bible to you.* You don't have to know homiletics and hermeneutics. You don't have to know Hebrew and Greek. You just have to know Jesus. That's it!

Now, I need to know homiletics and hermeneutics because I am called to be a teacher in the body of

Christ. The teacher you sit under in church will affect the way you read the Bible, but my job is not to teach you the Bible. My job is to teach you how to *study* the Bible. My job is to remove any obstacle you have so that when you read the Bible, Jesus can explain it to you. A pastor friend of mine who used to do a lot of counseling once told me, "Robert, it's my job to identify obstacles in people's lives in their relationship with Jesus and help them remove those obstacles so Jesus can speak to them." That's my job as a teacher in the body of Christ. If I see an obstacle of legalism trying to influence the church, my job is to teach about grace so that people can read the Bible through the lens of grace.

Look at Luke 24:27 in the Message:

> Then he started at the beginning, with the Books of Moses, and went on through all the Prophets, pointing out everything in the Scriptures that referred to him (MSG).

Jesus pointed out everything in the Scriptures that referred to Him. "Moses and all the Prophets" refers to the Old Testament. In fact, Moses wrote the first five books. "All the Prophets" refers to the major and minor prophets. That's the way people referred to the Bible in Jesus' day. When the New Testament talks about "Scripture says," it's almost always referring to the Old Testament. We often write that off because we read the Old Testament through the lens of the Law, but Jesus showed the disciples on the Emmaus Road the lens of grace. He showed how everything was pointing to the Messiah. He might have shown them a Scripture like Psalm 22:16–18:

> They pierced My hands and My feet;
> I can count all My bones.
> They look *and* stare at Me.
> They divide My garments among them,
> And for My clothing they cast lots.

The Roman soldiers pierced His hands and feet on the cross. None of His bones were broken. They cast lots for His clothing. These two disciples on the road to Emmaus might never have thought about that!

One of the benefits of the resurrection is that Jesus expounds and explains the Bible to you. The more you read the Bible, the more you will understand it and see Jesus in it. This makes sense because, after all, Jesus is the Author of the entire Bible.

It's not a book *written* by 40 different men. It was *penned* by 40 men, but there's one Author, and His name is Jesus. You don't have to go to seminary to understand the Bible. You just have to meet Jesus—the resurrected Christ—and He will explain the Scriptures to you.

HE OPENS

The two Emmaus Road disciples go back to the original 11 disciples and tell them that they saw Jesus. Then Jesus shows up again.

> Then He said to them, "These *are* the words which I spoke to you while I was still with you, that all things must be fulfilled which were written in the Law of Moses and *the* Prophets and *the* Psalms concerning Me." And He opened their understanding, that they might comprehend the Scriptures (Luke 24:44–45).

The word understanding is most often translated as 'mind,' and the word comprehend is most often translated as 'understand.' In the NIV, this reads: "Then he opened their minds so they could understand the Scriptures." Would it be okay with you if Jesus opened your mind—the way you think—so you could understand the Bible? Well, it's already happened! This is what the resurrected Christ did for all His disciples, and we are His disciples. Jesus has opened your eyes to understand the Word.

Here is verse 45 in the Message: "He went on to open their understanding of the Word of God, showing them how to read their Bibles this way." What is "this way"? The way you see Jesus on every page. Jesus showed His disciples every Scripture that referred to Him.

Remember, we talked about the difference between legalism and grace. If you don't read the Bible through the lens of grace, then you'll never understand it. Read it as a love story about God redeeming a sinful, fallen people. For example, God tells the prophet Hosea to marry a prostitute. But she goes back to prostitution, and then God tells Hosea to go get her and bring her back into his house. This is the same thing God has done for His people—for you and me! I really want you to fall in love with the *whole* Bible, not just the New Testament. The whole Book is incredible!

If you believe in Jesus, He's opened your mind, and now you can understand the Bible. But what if you don't believe in Jesus? According to the Bible, your mind has been blinded by the "god" of this world, Satan.

> But even if our gospel is veiled, it is veiled to those who are perishing, whose minds the god of this age has blinded, who do not believe, lest the light of the gospel of the glory of Christ, who is the image of God, should shine on them (2 Corinthians 4:3–4).

If you believe in Jesus, your mind is opened, and you can understand the Bible. If you don't believe in Jesus, then your mind is blinded, and you can't understand the Bible.

God always takes a truth and applies it a certain way for us. For example, how should we relate to people who don't believe in Jesus? How do we relate to people who vote differently than we vote and have different political leanings? Should we be angry, argue with them, or just leave them alone? Remember, the Bible says these people are spiritually blind. Using this analogy, consider a person who is visually impaired. Do you criticize or mock someone who carries a white cane? Or do you have empathy? If a visually impaired person bumps into you, do you become angry and attack them? No, you treat that person with kindness, because they can't see.

Likewise, you treat people who are so strong in their anti-Christ, anti-biblical opinions with love and compassion because they are blind. *They can't see.* The only reason we can see is because we believed in Jesus, and He opened our eyes (our understanding). Their understanding has not yet been opened.

I was greeting people in the church lobby one day, and a lady came up to Debbie and me. She was new to the church and liked the music and the message. She leaned in to say something softly to me: "Pastor Robert, I have a different view on something than you." And she told me what it was. With tears in her eyes, she said, "I just want to know if I'm welcome here." I immediately gave her a big hug. It was like a healing hug, and she started sobbing. I believe this woman had probably been treated really badly by others who had a different view than she did. I said, "You are very welcome here. I hope you come every week! I want you to come to everything we have."

Several months later, I was in the lobby once again. The same woman came up to me with a big smile on her face. She said, "Three weeks ago, I accepted Christ, and last week I got baptized." Then she leaned in and whispered, "And I changed my view on that thing we were talking about!"

HE BLESSES

Luke 24:50 says, "He led them out as far as Bethany, and He lifted up His hands and blessed them." What does it mean to be blessed? Many people relate this to finances, and I do believe God blesses us financially and provides for us. But I want to give you a different definition for being "blessed." I think it means that things just seem to work out. Almost all of us can give a testimony of being in the "right place at the right time." We can see the details and timing come together miraculously, as if Someone was planning it.

Jesus explains the Bible to us, opens our minds to understanding, and blesses us. But is there anything we can do as believers to stop this flow in our lives? Yes, there is. Luke 24 and Acts 1 record the ascension of Christ. Right before Jesus ascends, He has to adjust the disciples' thinking once again.

> Therefore, when they had come together, they asked Him, saying, "Lord, will You at this time restore the

kingdom to Israel?" And He said to them, "It is not for you to know times or seasons which the Father has put in His own authority. But you shall receive power when the Holy Spirit has come upon you; and you shall be witnesses to Me in Jerusalem, and in all Judea and Samaria, and to the end of the earth" (Acts 1:6–8).

These are the same disciples who spent 40 days with Jesus after the resurrection. He opened their understanding and explained the Scriptures to them. He blessed them. And then they asked, "Lord, are You now going to let us rule and reign? Are You going to restore the kingdom to us?" Jesus responds, *No! It is not about building your kingdom. It is about you building My kingdom!* Jesus is saying there are a whole bunch of people out there who don't know about the resurrected Christ. In other words, "What you need to do is go tell them about Me! Tell them I died for their sins and rose again. Go be My witnesses. Go build My kingdom."

What will stop the heavenly manna (Word of God that jumps off the page), the flow of water from the rock (the rock of revelation/comprehension), and the rain (blessings) from heaven is when you start to build your kingdom instead of God's kingdom. When you do that, it all stops!

There's something kind of neat in the 50 days from Passover to Pentecost that you may never have noticed. In Luke 24, it says the Emmaus Road disciples returned to "the eleven." In Acts 1, it says "the eleven" got together to choose another disciple, Matthias, to take Judas's place. Before the resurrection and after Pentecost the disciples were always referred to as "the twelve," but for the 50 days in-between, the original disciples were known as the "eleven." And that was because one guy (Judas) got concerned about building his own kingdom, and it was all downhill from there.

If you're a believer and the Bible is not jumping off the page anymore; if you don't understand what's going on in your life; if things don't seem to be working out ... then you might want to see if you're focused on building your kingdom instead of God's kingdom. You are not a bad human; it happens to everyone. And the solution is simple: repent. Matthew 6:33 says, "Seek first the kingdom of God and His righteousness, and all these things shall be added to you." When you repent, the Bible will start jumping off the page to you again, and you will start understanding what you're reading. You will be blessed so you can be a blessing to others.

NOTES

REFLECT

1. Did you grow up in a home where the Bible was read regularly? How did this affect you?

_____
_____
_____
_____
_____
_____

2. Read Luke 24:45. What do you think it means when it says Jesus "opened their understanding"? Whose understanding did Jesus open?

_____
_____
_____
_____
_____
_____

3. Have you ever had a Scripture stand out to you in a special way while reading the Bible? What was that experience like?

_____
_____
_____
_____
_____
_____
_____

4. What does it mean that Jesus is not only the Word but He also teaches us the Word?

_____
_____
_____
_____
_____
_____
_____

5. Why is it important to base our decisions on what the Word says rather than our thoughts, feelings, or emotions?

PRAY

Spend some time in prayer and ask the Holy Spirit, "What are You saying to me through this message?"

_____

_____

_____

_____

_____

_____

_____

_____

_____

_____

_____

_____

_____

_____

EXPLORE

KEY QUOTE

> *If you believe in Jesus, He's opened your mind, and now you can understand the Bible.*

How comfortable are you with your ability to read and understand the Bible?

_____

_____

_____

_____

_____

KEY VERSES

Luke 24:25–27, 44–45
2 Corinthians 4:3–4
Acts 1:6–8

What truths stand out to you as you read these verses?

_____
_____
_____

What is the Holy Spirit saying to you through these Scriptures?

_____
_____
_____

KEY QUESTION

Are you focused on building God's kingdom or your kingdom?

_____
_____
_____
_____
_____
_____

KEY PRAYER

Heavenly Father, thank You for giving us Your Word, the Bible. Help us to value it, study it, and allow it to change us. Help us to always come to You first and use the blessings You give us to build Your kingdom. In Jesus' name, Amen.

NOTES

_____
_____
_____
_____
_____
_____
_____
_____
_____
_____
_____

SESSION 4

BELIEVE

SESSION 4

BELIEVE

True faith is active. The disciples struggled with doubt, and Jesus needed to teach them how to have faith and believe. Jesus is God, He loves us, and we love Him even when we make a mistake.

ENGAGE

Did you find it easier to believe in things you could not see when you were a child? How has your ability to believe changed as you've gotten older?

_____

_____

_____

_____

_____

_____

_____

RECAP

In the previous message, we learned that Jesus explains the Scriptures to us. He opens our minds to the truth and blesses us so we can build His kingdom. Did you read the Word with a new perspective or more understanding last week?

WATCH

Watch "Believe." Think about the ways we believe in the Father, the Son, and the Holy Spirit. Consider how Jesus empowers us to believe.

> If you're unable to watch this message, skip to the Read section.

NOTES

READ

What was Jesus' purpose during the 40 days He was on the earth after the resurrection? Why did He spend so much time here? In the past two messages, we learned that He spent time teaching the disciples not to judge according to the flesh, explaining the Scriptures to them, and blessing them. To learn more about what Jesus did during these 40 days, read the last chapters of Matthew, Mark, Luke, and John.

During the 40 days, Jesus also spent time trying to get the disciples to *believe.* You may wonder, *Didn't they already believe?* Well, here are some Scriptures that prove otherwise:

> Now when *He* rose early on the first *day* of the week, He appeared first to Mary Magdalene, out of whom He had cast seven demons. She went and told those who had been with Him, as they mourned and wept. And when they heard that He was alive and had been seen by her, **they did not believe**.
> After that, He appeared in another form to two of them as they walked and went into the country. And they went and told *it* to the rest, *but* they did not believe them either (Mark 16:9–13, bold added).

Verse 11 says "They did not believe." "They" refers to the 11 original disciples. Verse 13 refers to the two disciples on the road to Emmaus. The 11 original disciples did not believe them either, and Jesus had spent three and a half years with them! How many times had Jesus told them what would happen? So why weren't the disciples at the tomb on the third day? *They didn't believe.* In Luke 24:10–11, several women told the disciples about Jesus' resurrection, and they did not believe them either. That's why He had to spend 40 more days on earth.

Let's look at three applications to "believe."

BELIEVE JESUS IS GOD

First, believe Jesus is God. He's not just the Son of God, but He's also God the Son. Here is a passage to help you understand how you can strengthen your belief. This occurs just after Jesus returns from the Mount of Transfiguration, where He was transfigured in front of Peter, James, and John. There were nine disciples at the bottom of the mountain.

> And when He came to the disciples, He saw a great multitude around them, and scribes disputing with

them. Immediately, when they saw Him, all the people were greatly amazed, and running to Him, greeted Him. And He asked the scribes, "What are you discussing with them?"

Then one of the crowd answered and said, "Teacher, I brought You my son, who has a mute spirit. And wherever it seizes him, it throws him down; he foams at the mouth, gnashes his teeth, and becomes rigid. So I spoke to Your disciples, that they should cast it out, but they could not."

He answered him and said, "O faithless generation, how long shall I be with you? How long shall I bear with you? Bring him to Me." Then they brought him to Him. And when he saw Him, immediately the spirit convulsed him, and he fell on the ground and wallowed, foaming at the mouth.

So He asked his father, "How long has this been happening to him?"

And he said, "From childhood. And often he has thrown him both into the fire and into the water to destroy him. But if You can do anything, have compassion on us and help us."

Jesus said to him, "If you can believe, all things *are* possible to him who believes."

Immediately the father of the child cried out and said with tears, "Lord, I believe; help my unbelief!" (Mark 9:14–24).

The first thing I want you to notice is how calm Jesus is when he says, "Bring him to Me" (v. 19). While the boy is convulsing, He calmly asks the father how long the boy has been like this. Jesus is not unconcerned with the boy—He is unimpressed with the demon. That's because Jesus is God! Then, when He sees people coming to see the demon's show, He casts out the demon.

Notice the "ifs" in this passage. The father says, "If you can do anything" (v. 22). Here is a paraphrase of Jesus' answer: "The question isn't *if I* can do anything. The question is '*if you*' can believe. Because I can do it." The man's answer—"Lord, I believe; help my unbelief"—is a great answer (v. 24). Like me, I'm sure many of you can relate to this father's plea.

Then Jesus gives the disciples the key to getting more belief:

> And when He had come into the house, His disciples asked Him privately, "Why could we not cast it out?"
> So He said to them, "This kind can come out by nothing but prayer and fasting" (vv. 28–29).

The disciples had already been given authority to cast out demons and had done so on many occasions, but here Jesus says the key to more faith is *action*! If you want to have more faith, then you have to press into God and *do something.*

There is a famous passage in James about faith and works:

> Wasn't our ancestor Abraham "made right with God by works" when he placed his son Isaac on the sacrificial altar? Isn't it obvious that faith and works are yoked partners, that faith expresses itself in works? That the works are "works of faith"? The full meaning of "believe" in the Scripture sentence, "Abraham believed God and was set right with God," includes his action. It's that weave of believing and acting that got Abraham named "God's friend" (James 2:21–23 MSG).

Faith is active, and Abraham *placing* Isaac on the altar is an example of active faith. In Romans chapter 4, Paul tells us that Abraham was made right with God by his faith. James then adds action to faith. These two points are complementary, not contradictory. They give us a fuller understanding. True faith works—it does something. You don't get saved because you do something, but you do something because you get saved. For example, you read your Bible, pray, tithe, and attend church because you're saved. (There's something about coming together and worshipping God that is so special!)

Pastor Jonathan Evans once told a story about how they installed motion lights at his church, because people left the room and didn't turn off the lights. He made the point that the power is always there, but the light doesn't come on until there is activity in the room. There's nothing wrong with the power of God, but the power of God is not turned on until there is activity in your life. You have to do something!

BELIEVE JESUS LOVES YOU

Many people have a problem believing Jesus loves them. In fact, I had that problem for years. I would say, "I don't understand why God would ever love me." A counselor finally told me, "Robert, God loves you because God *is* loving. It's not because you're loveable." Let me show you a disciple who understood that God is love:

> Now the first *day* of the week Mary Magdalene went to the tomb early, while it was still dark, and saw *that* the stone had been taken away from the tomb. Then she ran and came to Simon Peter, and to the other disciple, whom Jesus loved, and said to them, "They have taken

away the Lord out of the tomb, and we do not know where they have laid Him."

Peter therefore went out, and the other disciple, and were going to the tomb. So they both ran together, and the other disciple outran Peter and came to the tomb first (John 20:1–4).

John refers to Himself throughout his Gospel as "the disciple whom Jesus loved." John and Peter ran together to the tomb, but John outran Peter and arrived first. Now look at verse 8: "Then the other disciple, who came to the tomb first, went in also; and he saw and believed." *There was one of the 11 who believed.* The reason John believed was because he knew that Jesus loved him. John says many times that Jesus loved him:

- "Now there was leaning on Jesus' bosom one of His disciples, whom Jesus loved" (John 13:23).
- "When Jesus therefore saw His mother, and the disciple whom He loved standing by, He said to His mother, 'Woman, behold your son!'" (John 19:26).
- "Therefore that disciple whom Jesus loved said to Peter, 'It is the Lord!'" (John 21:7).
- "Then Peter, turning around, saw the disciple whom Jesus loved following, who also had leaned

on His breast at the supper, and said, 'Lord, who is the one who betrays You?'" (John 21:20).

John knew Jesus loved Him. However, I do think it's humorous that John wrote about winning the race to Jesus' tomb. It reminds me of when Moses wrote in Numbers 12:3: "Now the man Moses *was* very humble, more than all men who *were* on the face of the earth." Moses and John weren't being egotistical. They were led by the Holy Spirit, so everything they said was factual. It doesn't mean Jesus didn't love the other disciples. It just means John *knew* Jesus loved him.

By the way, John is the only Gospel writer who recorded the *eleventh commandment*: "Love one another" (see John 13:34; 15:12, 17;1 John 4:21). This commandment is known as Jesus' new commandment.

John lived to be over 100 years old, and he was the only one of the original 11 disciples who was *not* martyred. Matthew was killed with a sword. Phillip was hung. Peter was crucified upside down. James the lesser was thrown from the Temple and then beaten to death. James the great was beheaded.

Simon the zealot was crucified. Bartholomew was flayed to death with a whip. Thomas was stabbed with a spear. Thaddeus was killed with arrows. Andrew was whipped by seven soldiers and then crucified.

An attempt was made to kill John. The Roman Colosseum was filled with people, and the soldiers put John into a cauldron of burning oil. Instead of dying, though, he kept preaching the Gospel. When they pulled him out of the cauldron, they saw that he had suffered no harm. So they exiled John to the Island of Patmos, where he wrote the book of Revelation.

Now, let's take a look at the last verse from John's Gospel.

> And there are also many other things that Jesus did, which if they were written one by one, I suppose that even the world itself could not contain the books that would be written. Amen (John 21:25).

John could not have been referring to the last three and a half years Jesus was on this earth, because you could write a book about everything Jesus had done in that time. The only way you can understand the last verse of John's Gospel is to understand the first verse of John's Gospel, which says, "In the beginning" (John 1:1). By the way, this is the exact way Genesis starts. If you write everything Jesus has done since the beginning of time for every human being, the world could not contain the books. John knew Jesus was (and is) God.

BELIEVE YOU LOVE JESUS

So when they had eaten breakfast, Jesus said to Simon Peter, "Simon, *son* of Jonah, do you love Me more than these?"

He said to Him, "Yes, Lord; You know that I love You."

He said to him, "Feed My lambs."

He said to him again a second time, "Simon, *son* of Jonah, do you love Me?"

He said to Him, "Yes, Lord; You know that I love You."

He said to him, "Tend My sheep."

He said to him the third time, "Simon, *son* of Jonah, do you love Me?" Peter was grieved because He said to him the third time, "Do you love Me?"

And he said to Him, "Lord, You know all things; You know that I love You."

Jesus said to him, "Feed My sheep. Most assuredly, I say to you, when you were younger, you girded yourself and walked where you wished; but when you are old, you will stretch out your hands, and another will gird you and carry *you* where you do not wish." This He spoke, signifying by what death he would glorify God. And when He had spoken this, He said to him, "Follow Me" (John 21:15–19).

This conversation took place during the 40 days after Jesus' resurrection. Three times Jesus says, "Peter, do you love Me?"

Remember, Peter was the most human of all the disciples. When Jesus walked on the water, He said, "It is I." Peter replied, "If it's You …" On the Mount of Transfiguration, Jesus took Peter, James, and John with Him to see Him transfigured. Moses and Elijah also showed up and talked with Jesus. Peter said, "It's a good thing I'm here!" God then called down from heaven and said, "Hear Him [Jesus]." In other words, *Peter, shut up!*

And one day, Jesus asked His disciples, "Who do you say I am?" They stumbled around with silly answers, but Peter said, "You are the Christ, the Son of the living God" (Matthew 16:15–16). Jesus said that flesh and blood did not reveal this to Peter. It was the

Father in heaven. In other words, *It was a miracle that you got the answer right!*

Then at the Last Supper, Jesus said all the disciples were going to deny Him. Of course, Peter said he would never deny Jesus. Later, after Peter's denial and the resurrection, Jesus is trying to get Peter to believe that he loves Him, so He asks Peter three times, "Do you love Me?" Peter's last answer was, "Lord, You know all things." Of course, Jesus knew the answer. He was trying to get Peter to know that he loved Him. God never asks you a question to learn something. He asks you a question so that *you* can learn something. When God asked Adam where he was hiding, He knew where Adam was. He wanted Adam to learn something.

Because of the resurrection, you can love Jesus. One of the amazing things about God is that He never disqualifies us from loving Him. We've all denied Jesus at some point in our lives, whether through our words or our actions. You may have denied Him at school, at work, or somewhere else. Still, God always welcomes us to repent and return. He lets us love Him again! That is the incredible power of the resurrection.

NOTES

REFLECT

1. Read James 2:21–23. How does faith express itself through actions?

2. The father of the boy in Mark 9 told Jesus he believed, but then he asked Jesus to help his unbelief. Why is this a good thing to ask?

3. Explain how the power of God is not turned on until there is activity in your life. What are some practical ways this applies to you?

_____
_____
_____
_____
_____
_____
_____

4. Why do some people have a hard time believing Jesus loves them?

_____
_____
_____
_____
_____
_____
_____

5. Has there ever been a time when your actions or words denied Jesus? How did you repent and return to the Lord?

_____
_____
_____
_____
_____
_____
_____
_____
_____
_____
_____
_____
_____
_____
_____
_____
_____
_____

Pray

Spend some time in prayer and ask the Holy Spirit, "What are You saying to me through this message?"

EXPLORE

KEY QUOTE

> *True faith works.*
> *True faith does something.*

What are some things you can do to put your faith into action?

_____
_____
_____
_____
_____
_____

KEY VERSES

Mark 16:9-29
James 2:21-23
John 21:15-19

What truths stand out to you as you read these verses?

_____
_____
_____

What is the Holy Spirit saying to you through these Scriptures?

_____
_____
_____

KEY QUESTION

Why is it important for us to believe that Jesus still loves us and we still love Him even when we mess up?

_____
_____
_____
_____
_____

KEY PRAYER

Heavenly Father, we believe Jesus is God, and You sent Him to pay the price for our sins. Help our unbelief and help us put our faith into action. We believe You love us, and we declare how much we love You! In Jesus' name, Amen.

NOTES

SESSION 5

WAITING FOR THE PROMISE

SESSION 5

WAITING FOR THE PROMISE

Before Jesus ascended into heaven, He told His disciples to stay and wait for the promise. Waiting is hard, but God designed it as part of the process of life. We must wait, pray, and let God build our faith and hope in Him. His timing is always perfect.

ENGAGE

Have you ever had to wait for a promise to come true? How did the waiting feel?

_____

_____

_____

_____

_____

_____

_____

RECAP

In the previous message, we learned that true faith is active. We need to believe that Jesus is God, that Jesus loves us, and that we love Jesus—even when we mess up. How did you recognize God's love for you this week? How did you recognize and express your love for Him?

WATCH

Watch "Waiting for the Promise." Think about how difficult is to wait. Consider the benefits of waiting.

> If you're unable to watch this message, skip to the Read section.

NOTES

READ

Now that we know what happened during the 40 days after the Jesus' resurrection, let's look at the 10 days between Jesus' ascension and the outpouring of the Holy Spirit on Pentecost.

During those 10 days, the disciples were waiting for the promise of the Holy Spirit. All of us have waited for something or someone at some point in our lives. We've also waited on God from time to time. Sometimes it feels like we're waiting on God for a *very* long time, which is why it's important to understand this theological truth: God does not have a watch, but He's never late.

The last words of Jesus before He ascended were not the Great Commission as seen in Matthew and Mark. They were not the word "go." The last chapter of Luke and the first chapter of Acts record Jesus' last words right before He ascended. He told His disciples, "*Stay* and *wait*, until you are endued with power from on high." Because if you go before you get the power, nothing is going to happen. Here are the passages:

> Behold, I am sending the promise of my Father upon you. But stay in the city until you are clothed with power from on high (Luke 24:49 ESV).

> And being assembled together with *them,* He commanded them not to depart from Jerusalem, but to wait for the Promise of the Father, "which," *He said,* "you have heard from Me" (Acts 1:4).

How long were they to wait? Well, *we know* it was 10 days, but they didn't know how long they would be waiting. They had to sit tight and trust the Lord to fulfill His promise.

In this message, I'll answer the questions, "Why does God make us wait?" and "Why didn't Jesus stay all 50 days?" I'll also explain *where* the disciples waited and how they waited.

WHERE DID THEY WAIT?

It's partially true that the disciples waited in "the upper room." (This wasn't the same room where they had eaten the Last Supper with Jesus.) The 11 original disciples plus Matthias, the 70 (other followers of Jesus), and some women (including Mary, the mother of Jesus) were all there waiting together. Interestingly, this is the last time Mary is mentioned in the Bible. She was present for the birth of Christ *and* the birth of the Church.

Then they returned to Jerusalem from the mount called Olivet, which is near Jerusalem, a Sabbath day's journey. And when they had entered, they went up into the upper room where they were staying: Peter, James, John, and Andrew; Philip and Thomas; Bartholomew and Matthew; James *the son* of Alphaeus and Simon the Zealot; and Judas *the son* of James (Acts 1:12–13).

A Sabbath Day's journey was about three-quarters of a mile, but the disciples would have referred to it as about 1,000 steps (of 36 inches each). It was a made-up Sabbath law that simply illustrates the distance they walked.

But the disciples weren't in the upper room the whole time.

> And they worshiped Him, and returned to Jerusalem with great joy, and were continually in the temple praising and blessing God. Amen (Luke 24:52–53).

The Church met continually (frequently) in the temple and in the house. We also need both places of meeting. If you only have church in the temple (church building) one day a week and do not have church in your house the other six days, you're missing something. You're also missing something if you only have church in your house and not in the temple. We need both!

> So continuing daily with one accord in the temple, and breaking bread from house to house, they ate their food with gladness and simplicity of heart (Acts 2:46).
>
> And daily in the temple, and in every house, they did not cease teaching and preaching Jesus *as* the Christ (Acts 5:42).

They met in the temple, and they met in houses. But there is a deeper principle here that Jesus spoke of in Matthew 22:35–40:

> Then one of them, a lawyer, asked *Him a question,* testing Him, and saying, "Teacher, which *is* the great commandment in the law?"
>
> Jesus said to him, "You shall love the Lord your God with all your heart, with all your soul, and with all your mind." This is *the* first and great commandment. And *the* second *is* like it: "You shall love your neighbor as

yourself. On these two commandments hang all the Law and the Prophets."

The point of this passage can be summarized as relationship with God and relationship with godly people. The principle is that if you are waiting on a promise from God, whatever that may be—family, job, whatever—you must wait in relationship with God and in relationship with God's people. You must maintain your relationship with God and with God's people, or you might not keep waiting for the promise.

Dr. Henry Cloud gave an illustration once when he spoke at our church. He said, "When you land at the end of a flight and turn your cellphone back on, it often says, 'Searching ...' That means it's searching for a connection. In the same way, every human being comes out of the womb searching for a connection with God and with people." Jesus summed up the whole Bible with these two commandments: have a relationship with God and have a relationship with God's people (see Mark 12:29–31).

HOW DID THEY WAIT?
They waited in prayer.

These all continued with one accord in prayer and supplication, with the women and Mary the mother of Jesus, and with His brothers (Acts 1:14).

Prayer means to ask, and *supplication* means to ask intensely—to ask fervently and passionately. Prayer is simply communicating with God—presenting your petitions to Him and talking to Him. When you talk to Him, you release the burden you're carrying, but if you don't pray, you keep the burden.

The New Testament Church prayed passionately, fervently, and frequently. Here are just some of the examples in Acts:

Acts 7:55–60	Stephen prayed as he was being stoned.
Acts 8:14–17	Peter prayed for the Samaritans to receive the Holy Spirit.
Acts 9:11	Saul of Tarsus prayed after his conversion.
Acts 9:36–43	Peter prayed before he raised Dorcas from the dead.
Acts 10:1–4	Cornelius prayed that God would show him how to be saved.
Acts 10:9	Peter prayed, and God told him to answer Cornelius's prayer.

Acts 12:1–11	The believers prayed for Peter when he was in prison.
Acts 13:1–3	They fasted and prayed before sending out Barnabas and Paul.
Acts 16:13–14	They were praying, and God opened Lydia's heart.
Acts 16:16–18	On the way to prayer, Paul cast a demon out of a girl.
Acts 16:25	Paul and Silas were praying, and God opened the prison doors.
Acts 20:36; 21:5	Paul prayed for his friends before leaving them.
Acts 27:35	During a storm, Paul prayed for God's blessing.
Acts 28:8	After the storm, Paul prayed that God would heal a sick man.

Prayer was a major part of the New Testament Church. The farther we get from prayer, the farther we get from receiving the promise of the Holy Spirit. There is an initial receiving of the Holy Spirit, but there is also a continual receiving of the Holy Spirit in every situation we're going through in life. And it comes through prayer.

Here are more examples:

> When all the people were baptized, it came to pass that Jesus also was baptized; and **while He prayed**, the heaven was opened. And the Holy Spirit descended in bodily form like a dove upon Him, and a voice came from heaven which said, "You are My beloved Son; in You I am well pleased" (Luke 3:21–22), emphasis added.

Most people miss three important words: *while He prayed*.

> And when they had prayed, the place where they were assembled together was shaken; and they were all filled with the Holy Spirit, and they spoke the word of God with boldness (Acts 4:31).

The Holy Spirit comes when we pray. You may be thinking, *I already have the Holy Spirit.* Yes, you do, but you also *need* the Holy Spirit right now in some situation, and He is waiting to intervene in that situation.

It's clear throughout Scripture that heaven is waiting for one person on earth to agree with heaven so the Lord can step in. He is waiting on us. That's why we are commanded to pray continually and fervently (see Ephesians 6:18).

My wife, Debbie, and I have three adult children: Josh, James, and Elaine. Josh is our firstborn, and two years after he was born, we began praying about having another child. I thought we would have a daughter next. After Debbie and I prayed one night, the Holy Spirit spoke to me. He said, "One year from today, you will have a son. You are to name him James Robert (after James Robison and yourself), and his ministry will surpass both of your ministries put together. And the enemy will try to take his life, but I will save him." Josh had been a c-section, but we felt that James was supposed to be born at home. When James was born—one year to the day later—the umbilical cord was wrapped around his neck twice, and his coloring was blue. The midwife helped remove the cord, and James is alive and well today!

When God spoke to me, I didn't sit back and do nothing. No, I went to the Lord and prayed. So many times we think, *I've got a promise from God, so I don't need to do anything,* but that simply isn't true. We need to pray!

WHY DID THEY WAIT?

Why did Jesus make the disciples wait 10 days? By the way, they didn't know it would be 10 days. Jesus didn't tell them to wait for Pentecost, so they didn't know how long they would be waiting. So why does God make people wait? You can ask "why" about many things. *Why* did I lose my job? *Why* did he get sick? *Why* did this happen? *Why* didn't that happen? *Why* did someone die? *Why*?

There's a simple answer to the waiting question: sometimes He makes you wait because He's God. He knows more than you know. He is all knowing and all loving. He's making you wait for your good and to build your faith.

What is faith? Hebrews 11:1 says, "Now faith is the substance of things hoped for, the evidence of things not seen." Faith is hope that you can't see. Romans 8:24–25 says it this way: "For we were saved in this hope, but hope that is seen is not hope; for why does one still hope for what he sees? But if we hope for what we do not see, we eagerly wait for *it* with perseverance." Hope and wait are in the same sentence.

Lamentations 3:26 says,

> *It is* good that *one* should hope and wait quietly
> For the salvation of the Lord.

If you already have everything you want, then you actually have no hope. People who have everything don't hope for anything. So why does God want us to hope? He's building our faith.

The key to building your faith is building your relationship with God. He's given you a promise, but you can't handle the promise yet. He is building His relationship with you and your relationship with Him so that when the promise comes, you can handle it.

Remember, the promise was the power and the Person of the Holy Spirit. If you're not prepared for the power, then it can destroy you. The reason God made the disciples wait 10 days was so they would go deeper in their relationship with Him through prayer. They would get deep enough that when the power of the Holy Spirit came, they would be able to handle it.

Look at Abraham and Sarah: God made them wait 25 years for the promise of a son. Why? Because they wouldn't have been able to handle it. We know this because 11 years into it, Sarah gave her maid to Abraham to sleep with and try to accomplish the promise on their own. Sarah and Abraham were not ready to handle the promise.

Why did God tell Abraham and Sarah about their son 25 years before he would be born? Why not tell them one year before? Because it would take them 25 years of waiting, hoping, and praying to have enough maturity to handle it. Sometimes God makes you wait so you can handle the promise. He is building your faith—your relationship with Him—so that when the promise comes, you won't fail.

God's timing is always perfect. Abraham and Sarah named their son Isaac. One day, Abraham sent a servant to his brother's household to find a wife for Isaac. On that exact day, the servant arrives at a well, and Rebekah comes to the same well. If Isaac been born 25 years earlier, Rebekah would probably not have been born yet. God knows! He has every day of everyone's life planned perfectly!

Isaac and Rebekah had their son Jacob at the exact right time so that Jacob could meet Rachel, whose womb God opened at exactly the right time to have Joseph. And this continues all the way to a virgin named Mary. It's still continuing to this day, with your children and grandchildren. God is determining the days of their lives to perfection.

God ordained for Mary to be born at a certain time so that the angel could come to her at a certain time so that Jesus could be born on a certain day so that He could begin His ministry at 30 and die at 33 on Passover. Fifty days later, the Holy Spirit came at Pentecost on the exact day. And it started with Abraham and Sarah having to wait 25 years for the promise.

You are waiting for a promise, but it's important to know *where*, *how*, and *why* you need to wait. Where you need to wait is in relationship with God and with His people. How you need to wait is in prayer. And why you need to wait is because God is doing it for your good.

NOTHING CAN COMPARE WITH GOD'S TIMING.

Years ago, there was a young lady who had to repeat second grade due to her reading level not being advanced enough for third grade. There was also a boy who was born a few days before the cutoff date and was able to start school that year instead of waiting for the next year. The girl and the boy were supposed to be two grades apart, but they ended up in the same sixth-grade class. Forty-one years ago, they got married, and 21 years ago, they started a church in their living room called Gateway Church. Debbie and I are that boy and girl, and God worked everything out in our lives. He will work everything out in your life, too, if you will trust Him and wait for His promise.

NOTES

REFLECT

1. Why is waiting difficult?

_____
_____
_____
_____
_____
_____
_____

2. Why has God designed much of life to include waiting?

_____
_____
_____
_____
_____
_____
_____
_____

3. How does waiting on God deepen our relationship with Him?

_____

_____

_____

_____

_____

_____

_____

4. How are hope and faith connected?

_____

_____

_____

_____

_____

_____

_____

5. In what area of your life do you need a word of encouragement from the Holy Spirit? Take a moment to pray about this area.

_____
_____
_____
_____
_____
_____
_____
_____
_____
_____
_____
_____
_____
_____
_____

PRAY

Spend some time in prayer and ask the Holy Spirit, "What are You saying to me through this message?"

_____

_____

_____

_____

_____

_____

_____

_____

_____

_____

_____

_____

_____

_____

EXPLORE

KEY QUOTE

> *He is building His relationship with you and your relationship with Him so that when the promise comes, you can handle it.*

What is the one thing you will do to help build your relationship with God this week?

_____
_____
_____
_____
_____

KEY VERSES

Luke 24:49
Acts 1:4, 14; 5:42
Lamentations 3:26

What truths stand out to you as you read these verses?

_____

_____

_____

What is the Holy Spirit saying to you through these Scriptures?

_____

_____

_____

KEY QUESTION

How does waiting mature our faith?

_____

_____

_____

_____

_____

_____

KEY PRAYER

Heavenly Father, thank You for perfectly planning every day of our lives. Thank You that we can trust in You and Your love for us. Give us grace to wait for Your promises. We believe You love us and have good plans for us. In Jesus' name, Amen.

NOTES

_____
_____
_____
_____
_____
_____
_____
_____
_____
_____
_____

SESSION 6

PENTECOST

SESSION 6

PENTECOST

Pentecost was the celebration of the giving of the Law, and it occurred 50 days after Passover. Now Pentecost is the giving of the Spirit that brings life, not the giving of the Law that brought death.

ENGAGE

What is the greatest gift you've ever received? Was it expected or a surprise?

RECAP

In the previous message, we learned that while waiting can be hard, waiting for God's promises is an important part of building a believer's faith and relationship with God. What promise of God are you waiting on? How will you wait?

WATCH

Watch "Pentecost." Think about what Pentecost symbolized in the Old Testament. Consider what Pentecost means to believers today.

> If you're unable to watch this message, skip to the Read section.

NOTES

READ

Some people are scared by the word *Pentecost* because it sounds similar to the word *Pentecostal*. I was raised Baptist, but when I was eight years old, I attended a Pentecostal church service for the first time with my Aunt Prudie and Uncle Smokie. Things seemed completely normal until the music started. Then these "normal" adults went crazy! They began shouting, running around the sanctuary, and speaking in tongues. One guy even ran around during the pastor's message! It was a frightening experience for an eight-year-old boy. This was my first impression of the Pentecostal denomination, and my only thought was, *I do not want to be a Pentecostal when I grow up!*

I'm not saying anything negative about the Pentecostal denomination, but I realize some people might have had the same experience and, therefore, feel a little afraid or uncomfortable with this word. And if you feel that way, then it's possible you might feel the same way about the Person of the Holy Spirit. You might think, *I'm glad I invited Jesus into my life, but I don't really want to invite a Person who would make me lose my mind.*

WHAT IS PENTECOST?

The word Pentecost simply means "50." There is no reason to be scared of the word 50! Pentecost was the celebration of the giving of the Law at Mt. Sinai. It occurred 50 days after Passover, when God's people took the blood of the lamb and put it on their doorposts so the death angel would pass over their houses.

The New Testament Pentecost was 50 days after the resurrection. Passover was on Friday (when Jesus was crucified), then the Sabbath came, and finally there were 50 days until Pentecost. That's 50 days plus two more. So how did that change from the Old Testament? God changed it back in Leviticus 23:15–16:

> And you shall count for yourselves from the day after the Sabbath, from the day that you brought the sheaf of the wave offering: seven Sabbaths shall be completed. Count fifty days to the day after the seventh Sabbath; then you shall offer a new grain offering to the Lord.

The new grain offering was to be offered after seven weeks plus a day (the Feast of Weeks) after the first *Sabbath* after the Passover, so that the celebration of Pentecost would match up with the time after the Messiah's resurrection. God knew His Son would rise the day after that Sabbath. That's why we see in Acts 2:1 the phrase, "When the day of Pentecost had fully come." "Fully" means 50 days after the Sabbath.

Do you see how wonderful God is? When the Law was given, there was a sound from heaven, God wrote His Law on tablets of stone, and 3,000 people died. At the giving of the Spirit, there was a sound from heaven, God wrote His Law on tablets of flesh (people's hearts), and 3,000 people were saved! The Law brings death; the Spirit brings life. God works all this out perfectly.

WHAT HAPPENED AT PENTECOST

To understand what happened at Pentecost, we need to go back to the Old Testament again:

> For then I will restore to the peoples a pure language,
> That they all may call on the name of the Lord,
> To serve Him with one accord (Zephaniah 3:9).

"Then" refers to when the Messiah comes. "Peoples" refers to nations. Note particularly the phrase "one accord." God will restore to the nations a pure language so they can worship Him in one accord.

Also notice "a pure language." Every language in the world has curse words and dirty words in it. A pure language refers to the language of heaven, where there will be no dirty, impure, or immoral words.

The *main* word I want you to see here is "restore." God says He is going to *bring back* a pure language. If so, when did He take it away? Genesis 11 tells the story of the Tower of Babel. Babel means 'confusion.' (Babylon means 'sown or planted in confusion.')

Before the Tower of Babel, all the people spoke one language (not Hebrew, since Israel was not established yet). God is going to bring back a pure language.

> Now the whole earth had one language and one speech. And it came to pass, as they journeyed from the east, that they found a plain in the land of Shinar, and they dwelt there. Then they said to one another, "Come, let us make bricks and bake *them* thoroughly." They had brick for stone, and they had asphalt for mortar. And they said, "Come, let us build ourselves a city, and a tower whose top *is* in the heavens; let us make a name

for ourselves, lest we be scattered abroad over the face of the whole earth."

But the Lord came down to see the city and the tower which the sons of men had built. And the Lord said, "Indeed the people *are* one and they all have one language, and this is what they begin to do; now nothing that they propose to do will be withheld from them. Come, let Us go down and there confuse their language, that they may not understand one another's speech." So the Lord scattered them abroad from there over the face of all the earth, and they ceased building the city (Genesis 11:1–8).

I would have thought the Lord would have told them, "Good luck on building a tower to heaven. That's not going to happen." But in verse 6, He says they *could* do it. With one language, if they were in one accord, it would have been possible. *Nothing would be withheld from them if they had this language and were in unity.* In Zephaniah, God said He would restore—bring back—the pure language He had taken away.

God said to let Us—Father, Son, and Holy Spirit—go down and confuse their language so they can't understand each other. On the day of Pentecost, the Holy Spirit came down, and everyone could understand each other. The Lord scattered them from Babel, but in Acts 2, the Lord gathered them together! Now let's look at Acts 2:

> When the Day of Pentecost had fully come, they were all with one accord in one place. And suddenly there came a sound from heaven, as of a rushing mighty wind, and it filled the whole house where they were sitting....
>
> And there were dwelling in Jerusalem Jews, devout men, from every nation under heaven. And when this sound occurred, the multitude came together, and were confused, because everyone heard them speak in his own language (vv. 1–2, 5–6).

Pentecost is not just the blessed reversal of the giving of the Law (because the Law brings death, and the Spirit brings life). Pentecost is also the blessed reversal of the Tower of Babel. At the Tower of Babel, they were all in unity and spoke one language, but they weren't redeemed by the blood of Jesus. Therefore, their hearts and purposes were wicked. God scattered them until after His Son died on the cross for their sins. Then He would redeem them and bring them back together as well as bring this language back.

CAN I EXPERIENCE PENTECOST?

There is a popular line of thought in the Church that Pentecost was a one-time event that none of us can experience because we weren't there 2,000 years ago.

Instead of saying it "happened," I would rather say Pentecost was *fulfilled* 2,000 years ago, in the same way Passover was fulfilled 2,000 years ago. We don't have to shed the blood of a lamb for our sins because the Lamb from heaven came. Even though we weren't alive then, we can still experience the fulfillment of Passover by receiving Jesus into our lives. Likewise, we can experience the fulfillment of Pentecost by receiving the Holy Spirit into our lives.

Peter gets up and explains all of this to the people in Acts 2. Here is their response:

> Now when they heard *this,* they were cut to the heart, and said to Peter and the rest of the apostles, "Men *and* brethren, what shall we do?"
>   Then Peter said to them, "Repent, and let every one of you be baptized in the name of Jesus Christ for the remission of sins; and you shall receive the gift of the

Holy Spirit. For the promise is to you and to your children, and to all who are afar off, as many as the Lord our God will call" (Acts 2:37–39).

Peter tells them to do three things: repent, be baptized, and receive the gift of the Holy Spirit. Jesus called the gift the *promise* in Acts 1. In verse 39, Peter makes it clear that the promise was not just for then but is also for now. Not just for you but also for your children and grandchildren. Two examples in Acts (among others) demonstrate this:

> But when they believed Philip as he preached the things concerning the kingdom of God and the name of Jesus Christ, both men and women were baptized. Then Simon himself also believed; and when he was baptized he continued with Philip, and was amazed, seeing the miracles and signs which were done.
>
> Now when the apostles who were at Jerusalem heard that Samaria had received the word of God, they sent Peter and John to them, who, when they had come down, prayed for them that they might receive the Holy Spirit. For as yet He had fallen upon none of them. They had only been baptized in the name of the Lord Jesus. Then they laid hands on them, and they received the Holy Spirit (Acts 8:12–17).

> And it happened, while Apollos was at Corinth, that Paul, having passed through the upper regions, came to Ephesus. And finding some disciples he said to them, "Did you receive the Holy Spirit when you believed?"
>
> So they said to him, "We have not so much as heard whether there is a Holy Spirit."
>
> And he said to them, "Into what then were you baptized?"
>
> So they said, "Into John's baptism."
>
> Then Paul said, "John indeed baptized with a baptism of repentance, saying to the people that they should believe on Him who would come after him, that is, on Christ Jesus."
>
> When they heard *this,* they were baptized in the name of the Lord Jesus. And when Paul had laid hands on them, the Holy Spirit came upon them, and they spoke with tongues and prophesied (Acts 19:1–6).

Acts 19 occurred 24 years after Acts 2. The apostles clearly knew that the believers needed to be baptized appropriately and receive the gift of the Holy Spirit. *Again, this is 24 years after Pentecost.*

Don't be concerned about the Holy Spirit because you have seen some weird things. Jesus said He would send us a Comforter, a *paracletos,* who would come alongside us.

My friend Peter Lord was a well-known Baptist pastor who wrote a book called *Turkeys and Eagles,* and his point was this: if God made you an eagle, why would you walk like a turkey? Peter went to be with the Lord at 91 years old. Before his death, Peter was having his quiet time with the Lord one day and reading his Bible. He came across Acts 19:2: *Have you received the Holy Spirit since you believed?* (KJV paraphrase). The Lord said to him, "Peter, have you received the Holy Spirit *since* you believed?" Peter tried to give God a theological answer: "Well, when I received Jesus, I received the Holy Spirit. He lives in my house." The Lord replied, "Well, your mother-in-law came to live with you 18 months ago. Have you received her?" Peter answered honestly, "No, I haven't." God said, "A lot of My children haven't received the Holy Spirit."

My burden for this message is not for hundreds or even thousands of people to receive the Holy Spirit. My burden is for *everyone* to receive the Holy Spirit. Imagine what it would be like if we all received the Holy Spirit and came together in unity!

NOTES

REFLECT

1. What did you think the word Pentecost meant before you heard or read this message? What is your understanding of the word Pentecost now?

_____

_____

_____

_____

_____

_____

2. Read Acts 19:2. What were you taught about the Holy Spirit up until now?

_____

_____

_____

_____

_____

_____

3. Why do you think some people are afraid of the Holy Spirit?

_____

_____

_____

_____

_____

_____

_____

4. What has been your experience with the Holy Spirit?

_____

_____

_____

_____

_____

_____

_____

5. What does it mean to *receive* the Holy Spirit? How do we receive the Holy Spirit?

_____
_____
_____
_____
_____
_____
_____
_____
_____
_____
_____
_____
_____
_____
_____
_____

PRAY

Spend some time in prayer and ask the Holy Spirit, "What are You saying to me through this message?"

_____

_____

_____

_____

_____

_____

_____

_____

_____

_____

_____

_____

_____

_____

_____

EXPLORE

KEY QUOTE

> *Imagine what it would be like if we all received the Holy Spirit and came together in unity!*

Do you feel in one accord with other believers? What about with the Holy Spirit?

_____
_____
_____
_____
_____
_____

KEY VERSES

Zephaniah 3:9
Genesis 11:6–8
Acts 2:1–6

What truths stand out to you as you read these verses?

_____
_____
_____

What is the Holy Spirit saying to you through these Scriptures?

_____
_____
_____

KEY QUESTION

Have you received the Holy Spirit since you believed?

_____
_____
_____
_____
_____

KEY PRAYER

Dear Jesus, we ask You to baptize us today with the Holy Spirit. Holy Spirit, I ask You to forgive me for having preconceived thoughts and attitudes about You that were incorrect. As an act of my will and in faith, I receive You, Holy Spirit, fully in my life. In Jesus' name, Amen.

NOTES

LEADER'S GUIDE

Thank you so much for serving as a small group/class leader for this sermon series. God has amazing things planned for everyone involved, including you! The following guide shares some best practices for a life-changing, interactive experience.

BEFORE YOU MEET
- Ask God to prepare the hearts and minds of the people in your small group or class. Ask Him to show you how to encourage each person to integrate the principles found in these messages into their daily lives through group discussion and journaling.
- Watch the message for the week.
- Plan how much time you'll give to each portion of your meeting (see the suggested schedule below). In case you're unable to get through all the activities in the time allotted, choose two questions from the **Talk** section from each message.

SUGGESTED SCHEDULE

1. **Engage** and **Recap** (5 Minutes)
2. **Watch** or **Read** (20 Minutes)
3. **Reflect** (25 Minutes)
4. **Pray** (10 minutes)

KEY TIPS FOR THE LEADER

- Generate participation and discussion.
- Resist the urge to teach. The goal is for great conversation that leads to discovery.
- Ask open-ended questions—questions that can't be answered with "yes" or "no" (e.g., "What do you think about that?" rather than "Do you agree?").
- When a question arises, ask the participants for their input first, instead of immediately answering it yourself.
- Be comfortable with silence. If you ask a question and no one responds, rephrase the question, and wait for a response. Your primary role is to create an environment where the participants feel comfortable to be themselves and engage, not to provide the answers to all their questions.
- Ask the participants to pray for each other from week to week, especially about key issues that arise during your time together. This is how you begin to build authentic community and

encourage spiritual growth within the small group/class.

KEYS TO A DYNAMIC SMALL GROUP

RELATIONSHIPS

Meaningful, encouraging relationships are the foundation of a dynamic small group. Teaching, discussion, worship, and prayer are important elements of a group meeting, but the depth of each element is often dependent upon the depth of the relationships among members.

AVAILABILITY

Building a sense of community within your small group requires members to prioritize their relationships with one another. This means being available to listen, care for one another, and meet each other's needs.

MUTUAL RESPECT

Mutual respect is shown when small group members value each other's opinions (even when they disagree) and are careful never to put down or embarrass others in the group (including their spouses, who may or may not be present).

OPENNESS

A healthy small group environment encourages sincerity and transparency. Members treat each other with grace in areas of weakness, allowing each other room to grow.

CONFIDENTIALITY

To develop authenticity and a sense of safety within the group, each small group member must be able to trust that things discussed within the group will not be shared outside the group. (What's said in the group stays in the group.)

SHARED RESPONSIBILITY

Small group members should share the responsibility by using their God-given abilities to serve at each meeting. Some may greet, some may host, some may teach, etc. Ideally, each person should be available to care for others as needed.

SENSITIVITY

Dynamic small groups are born when the leader consistently seeks and is responsive to the guidance of the Holy Spirit, following His leading throughout the meeting as opposed to sticking to the "agenda." This guidance is especially important during the discussion and prayer time.

FUN!

Dynamic small groups take the time to have fun. Create an atmosphere for fun and be willing to laugh at yourself every now and then!

ROBERT MORRIS

Robert Morris is the senior pastor of Gateway Church, a multicampus church based in Dallas-Fort Worth, Texas. Since it began in 2000, the church has grown to more than 100,000 active attendees. His television program airs in over 190 countries, and his radio program, *Worship & the Word with Pastor Robert*, airs in more than 2,800 radio markets across America. He serves as chancellor of The King's University and is the best-selling author of numerous books, including *The Blessed Life*, *Frequency*, *Beyond Blessed*, and *Take the Day Off*. Robert and his wife, Debbie, have been married 42 years and are blessed with one married daughter, two married sons, and nine grandchildren.

PastorRobert.com

GET THE VIDEO SERIES

Purchase the companion video series at
GatewayPublishing.com

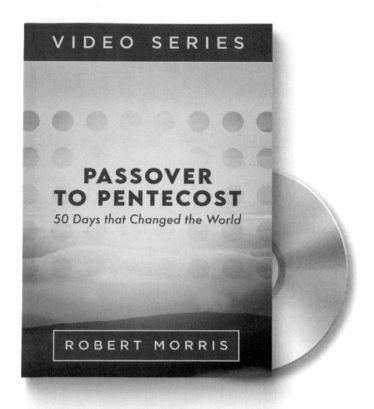

DISCOVER MORE
SERMON SERIES

The Blessed Life *The God I Never Knew*

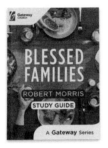 

Blessed Families *The End ...*

Living in His Presence *More Than Words*

Explore all available series at
GatewayPublishing.com

ALSO FROM
ROBERT MORRIS

Dream to Destiny

A Proven Guide to Navigating Life's Biggest Tests and Unlocking Your God-Given Purpose

Newly revised and expanded edition! Drawing on the biblical story of Joseph, Robert Morris shares exactly how to step into your purpose. Why settle for a dream when you can have the destiny?

The Blessed Life

Unlocking the Rewards of Generous Living

When God changes your heart from selfishness to generosity, every part of your life journey is affected. With humor, passion, and clarity, Robert presents this truth.

How Do I Know?

Do you want to learn more about the reality of God? The truth of the Bible? The person of Jesus? Pastor Robert Morris answers your questions.

GatewayPublishing.com

FRESH START BIBLE

Everyone needs help navigating their way through life. Pastor Robert Morris and other key leaders answer common questions and provide the tools for building a strong spiritual foundation. With over 500 discipleship articles and studies, *Fresh Start Bible* will help you find God's direction for every day.

AVAILABLE EDITIONS:

Softcover Linen
Hardcover Linen
Deluxe Edition (Imitation Leather)
Premium Edition (Genuine Leather)
Large Print Edition (Imitation Leather)
Spanish Edition (Imitation Leather)
Correctional Edition – for Prison Ministry (Softcover)
Ministry Edition – lowest cost (Paperback)

GatewayPublishing.com   FreshStartBible.com

New Living Translation, NLT, and the New Living Translation logo are registered trademarks of Tyndale House Publishers, Inc.